GOD MADE ME
UNIQUE

Helping Children See Value in Every Person

New Growth Press, Greensboro, NC 27404
Text Copyright © 2019 by Joni and Friends
Illustration Copyright © 2019 by Trish Mahoney

Unless otherwise indicated, Scripture quotations are taken from the New International Reader's Version (NIRV), Copyright © 1995, 1996, 1998, 2014 by Biblica, Inc.®. Used by permission. All rights reserved worldwide.

ASL Friend definition Copyright © Baby Sign Language. http://www.babysignlanguage.com. Used by permission.

Art and Design: Trish Mahoney
Writer: Chonda Ralston

ISBN: 978-1-948130-70-7

Library of Congress Cataloging-in-Publication Data
Names: Joni and Friends, Inc.
Title: God made me unique : helping children see value in every person /
  Joni and Friends.
Description: Greensboro : New Growth Press, 2019.
Identifiers: LCCN 2019022014 | ISBN 9781948130707 (trade cloth)
Subjects: LCSH: Self-esteem--Religious aspects--Christianity--Juvenile
  literature. | Identity (Psychology)--Religious
  aspects--Christianity--Juvenile literature. | Respect for
  persons--Juvenile literature.
Classification: LCC BV4571.3 .G63 2019 | DDC 248.8/64--dc23
LC record available at https://lccn.loc.gov/2019022014

Printed in Canada

28 27 26 25 24 23 22 21   4 5 6 7 8

GOD MADE ME
UNIQUE

Helping Children See Value in Every Person

Joni and Friends

Foreword by
Joni Eareckson Tada

Illustrated by
Trish Mahoney

Written by
Chonda Ralston

"LORD, you are our Father.
We are the clay. You are the potter.
Your hands made all of us."

Isaiah 64:8

Dear Parent or Caregiver,

Thank you for taking the time to read *God Made Me Unique* to your child. This book was written to help you teach your children that God creates each unique individual and that disability is sometimes part of his plan, whether as a result of a condition from birth, or an injury or illness. We want children to understand that every person is made in the image of God and has tremendous value, regardless of their appearance or abilities.

I'm Joni Eareckson Tada, and when I was seventeen years old I broke my neck in a diving accident that left me a quadriplegic. I struggled initially, trying to comprehend how such a tragedy could be part of God's plan for me. Thanks to the love of our heavenly Father and the support of family and friends, I was able to grasp a different perspective on my disabilities and a renewed sense of purpose for my life. In 1979, I started Joni and Friends to advocate for those with disabilities and to help the church better understand how to come alongside families affected by disability.

We want to help eliminate fear and misconceptions about those who have special needs and emphasize the fact that every person deserves to be treated with kindness and respect. In this story, the children are encouraged to ask questions and gain an understanding about their new friend with a disability. We believe an open dialogue can help children replace harsh words and cold stares with honest questions and empathy. If you have this book in your hands, then you've already taken a step in the right direction and I applaud you ... for caring about those affected by disability and for being willing to teach your child a better way to interact with others. In the back of the book you'll find additional information and resources to equip you.

Cheering for you,

Joni

It all started as an ordinary Sunday at church...

Some children came yawning and rubbing their eyes.
None of them knew there would be a surprise.

Garrett was cranky. Jenna had the wiggles.
Ms. Campbell clapped to silence their giggles.

"I have an announcement, you'll all want to hear.
Please come join our circle; let's all gather near."

Ms. Campbell sat waiting as children grew quiet.
They all sat down slowly; that is, except Wyatt.

He stood in the back with a small spinning toy;
His mom always says he's a busy young boy.

The toy helps him focus—keep hands to himself.
Ms. Campbell keeps extras up high on her shelf.

"Thank you for giving me all your attention.
Before we get started there's news I will mention."

"There's a friend who is joining our class this week.
Our friend's name is Brie and like us, she's unique.

Her family moved here just two weeks ago.

She loves to eat pizza;
her dog's name is Bo.

First days can be hard when all things are brand new.
Like the first day of school, do you think this is true?"

"I cried when I started first grade," said Jamal.
"They looked right at my chair and said I couldn't play ball."

"It hurts to be left out," Ms. Campbell agreed.
"We should never exclude based on a disability."

"We're all here this morning to talk about

special needs.

Have you heard of that phrase?
Do you know what it means?"

"I do!"
called out Wyatt,
while waving his hand.
"God made me unique, it was part of his plan."

"Thanks, Wyatt,"
Ms. Campbell said with a kind nod.

"You're right, we're all created
uniquely by God.

Brie's parents have asked
that I share news with you.

She has some special needs
to be aware of—just a few."

"Sometimes we call disabilities 'special needs.'
Some are quite clear and some others are unseen.

You have friends who use
braces to help their legs walk.

Or friends who are deaf
and use their hands to talk.

ASL (American Sign Language)

To make the sign for friend, hold out both of your index
fingers hooked in a C-shape. Holding one hand with your
C facing up, hook the second C into the first. Then reverse
the position for the hands and do it again. It is like your
fingers are best friends and giving each other a hug.

FRIEND

Jamal uses his wheelchair
to help him go fast.

Have you heard him beep as he buzzes past?"

BEEP!

BEEP!!

"Brie doesn't like some sounds
or loud noises she hears.

So she often wears headphones
to cover her ears."

Laticia's arm raised in the air rather quick.
"Is there something wrong? Is our new friend Brie sick?"

"Disabilities aren't germs that you're able to share.
They are part of creation, there's no need to be scared.

God made us, we read in Psalm one-thirty-nine.
He made us unique; we're all one-of-a-kind.

God, our Creator, made us with great care.
He planned every feature from our toes to our hair."

"You put me together inside my mother's body."
Psalm 139:13

"He even counts every hair on your head!"
Matthew 10:30

A knock on the door
brought Ms. Campbell to her feet.

Returning, she said,
"Class, here's someone to meet."

Brie's mom gently removed headphones
and then turned to go.

Ms. Campbell said,
"Friends, can you please wave hello?

Please join in the circle, we'll continue our lesson.
The Bible is where we find answers to our questions.

We were talking about how God made us unique.
From the tops of our heads
to the soles of our feet."

"Did you know that to balance, big toes play a part?
And tiny veins carry the blood to our heart?"

"The eyes," remarked Jenna, "help us see where to walk.
And if we had no tongue, we could not even talk.

Thank you!

We can't get a drink
without lifting the cup.

To bite into a cookie,
my hand picks it up."

"As it is, there are many parts. But there is only one body.
The eye can't say to the hand, 'I don't need you!'
The head can't say to the feet, 'I don't need you!'"

1 Corinthians 12:20-21

Ms. Campbell was excited,
"Isn't it neat?

All the parts work together
to make the body complete.

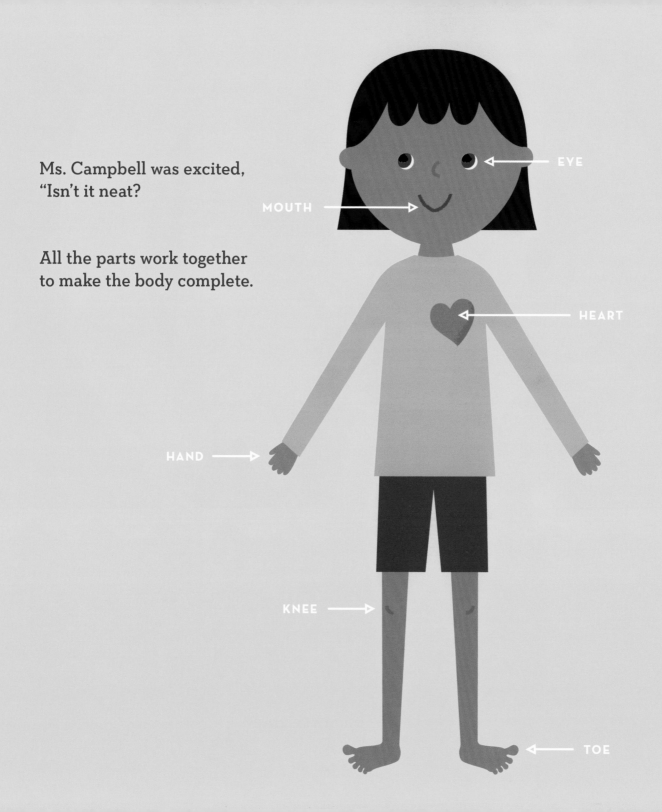

EYE

MOUTH

HEART

HAND

KNEE

TOE

Paul teaches that churches work in the same way. Every member has value and a part to play."

Jamal laughed, "Even if some parts don't work right! We're still important to God and never out of his sight."

"The parts of the body that seem to be weaker are the ones we can't do without. The parts that we think are less important we treat with special honor."

1 Corinthians 12:22–23

"God gifts us all with
unique talents to bring.

Some like to pray
and some others can sing.

There are those who make coffee
and pastors who preach.
There are members like me, who are able to teach."

"My mom rocks the babies on Sunday," Anne said.
"She prays for each one and then kisses their head."

"No service at church is too big or too small. We want everyone here.

God uses us all."

"Our class time will quickly come to a close.
Do you have any questions or things you don't know?"

Sammy, a shy boy, then raised up his hand.
"My brother has special needs—I understand."

"I'm so glad this lesson has helped you to see.
Disabilities are part of how God made us unique.

Let's pray and thank God for teaching us about our worth."

And a small voice said,

"God, thank you for making me feel welcome at church."

"Anyone who welcomes a
little child like this one in
my name welcomes me."

Matthew 18:5

Four Ways
to Help Your Child
Understand Uniqueness
and Disability as
Part of God's Plan

1 Teach your children that regardless of our abilities, we were each created by God with special value and gifts to share within our churches.

In the story, Ms. Campbell taught from 1 Corinthians 12:20-23, where the apostle Paul compared believers to the parts of a body that need each other to function properly. Paul summarized this message again in Romans. Review these verses to help your children appreciate their own uniqueness and see God's plan to use every person's gifts within their church family. We tend to recognize those who can sing, or preach, or serve in a high-profile position, but as Ms. Campbell pointed out: no act of service is "too big or too small."

"Each of us has one body with many parts. And the parts do not all have the same purpose. So also we are many persons. But in Christ we are one body. And each part of the body belongs to all the other parts. We all have gifts." Romans 12:4-6

2 Teach your children what the Bible says about God creating disability.

In the Old Testament we see that Moses had a disability. He was unable to speak clearly and may have stuttered. Because of his speech impairment, Moses didn't feel confident that God could use him to help free the Israelites from Pharaoh. But God makes it clear that he is our Creator and he would use Moses for his divine purpose.

"The Lord said to him, "Who makes human beings able to talk? Who makes them unable to hear or speak? Who makes them able to see? Who makes them blind? It is I, the Lord." Exodus 4:11

3   Teach your child about how Jesus responded to those with disabilities.

In Luke 14:21-23, Jesus teaches that we are to intentionally include people affected by disability in our lives. He showed great compassion for their pain and struggles, and throughout Scripture we see him healing people with disabilities.

Matthew 9:35 says that as Jesus went through the towns and villages teaching and preaching, he also healed many people.

In John 9:1-7 Jesus healed a man who had been blind since birth. He tells his disciples that the man's disability was part of God's plan because his healing displayed God's amazing power.

4   Teach your child about how to be a friend to someone with a disability.

In biblical times many people saw disability as a curse or a result of sin. Sadly, many people still have wrong beliefs about disability today. You can help your child see that Jesus wants us to love each other as God loves us. We can express love through friendship by not using words that are hurtful or not excluding people with disabilities.

In Mark 2:1-12 Jesus healed a man who couldn't walk. The man's friends carried him on a stretcher to seek help from Jesus. They even tore a hole in the roof of the building and lowered their friend down. Jesus praised their faith and efforts on behalf of their friend.

On the Joni and Friends website, Kids' Corner is Joni's special spot where children can learn how to be a better friend to someone with a disability. It's also a place where parents, teachers, and church leaders have access to free resources which help kids learn, grow, and serve. Both children and adults can learn about inspiring service projects, discover fun activities, and watch insightful videos, all to encourage relationships with those affected by disability.

www.joniandfriends.org/kids-corner